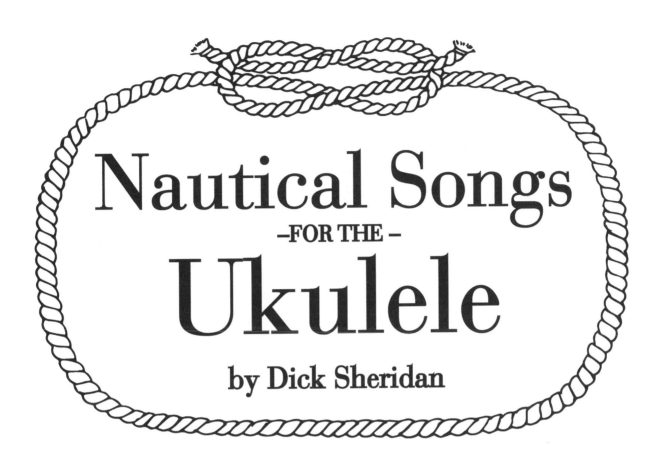

Nautical Songs
– FOR THE –
Ukulele

by Dick Sheridan

ISBN 978-1-57424-305-5
SAN 683-8022

Cover by James Creative Group

Copyright © 2014 CENTERSTREAM Publishing, LLC
P.O. Box 17878 - Anaheim Hills, CA 92817

www.centerstream-usa.com

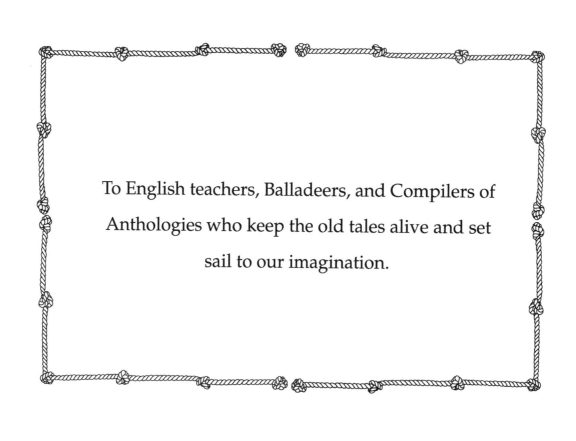

To English teachers, Balladeers, and Compilers of
Anthologies who keep the old tales alive and set
sail to our imagination.

Table of Contents

An Introduction

From earliest times, songs, tales, and legends of the sea have fascinated us and captured our imagination with vivid imagery. Folk songs old and new recall adventures on the high seas and the hazards of the deep. Chanteys describe workaday shipboard life – hoisting sails, hauling anchors, toting cargo, swabbing decks, climbing the riggings. Narrative ballads bring alive voyages doomed by storms, fogs, and shipwrecks. Fanciful lyrics summon pictures of buccaneer pirates, talking mermaids, bosun mates playing hop scotch with the crew, and girls who comb their hair with cod fish bones.

Life at sea was anything but glamorous. Danger was a constant threat. Whaling was treacherous with longboats overturned by the flip of a whale's fluke or a furious "Nantucket sleigh ride." Accidents occurred climbing the riggings and ratlines, and there was always the dreaded cry of "Man overboard!" Infractions of ship's rule brought harsh punishments – keelhauling, walking the plank, floggings with a cat-o-nine-tails. Food could be poor and rations were slim. Understandably, mutinies were not uncommon.

Long periods at sea brought longings for home and loved ones. Back on shore after a voyage of many months, sailors wasted no time in resuming courtships or augmenting the limited ration of grog doled out on shipboard. On land a sailor's swagger might come from sea legs acquired on a ship's rolling deck – or more likely from a drop too many at the waterfront wharf tavern.

Always eager for a good sea yarn not only in song but in prose, verse, on the stage or in the movies, the public has been amply rewarded with such works as Herman Melville's *Billy Budd* and *Moby Dick* (now an opera!) Richard Henry Dana's *Two Years Before the Mast*, Ernest Hemmingway's *The Old Man and The Sea*, Walt Disney's *Pirates of the Caribbean*, and Nordhoff & Hall's *Mutiny on the Bounty*. Let's not forget the German maiden, *Lorelei*, who with her beauty and song lured sailors to their doom on the rocks of the River Rhine.

Not to be overlooked are tales of notorious pirates, real or fictional, like Captain Kidd, Blackbeard, Long John Silver from Robert Louis Stevenson's *Treasure Island*, Captain Hook from *Peter Pan*, and Grace O'Malley, the legendary pirate queen.

Gilbert & Sullivan's comic operas tell of The Pirates of Penzance, the "Ruler of the Queen's Navee" who has never been to sea, and a ship's captain who never gets seasick – well, hardly ever.

But not all nautical literature, musical or otherwise, is linked to the open ocean. There's plenty of activity on shore and along the inland waterways. Paddle-wheelers churn the Mississippi. Farmers hide their hogs and chickens – and surely their daughters – when roustabouts come ashore. Rowboat lotharios romance their sweeties, and love songs can be heard on moonlit bays. Swimmers frolic in the surf, waterfalls tumble, and sailors drop their sea bags to dance a hornpipe or two.

All of this and so much more is reflected in the songs that follow. There's patriotism and an international flavor with songs about rivers in Scotland and Ireland, a lake in the Scottish highlands, a Neapolitan boat song from Italy, a favorite Australian chantey, a calypso favorite from the Caribbean, and from Greenland a rollicking good ditty about whaling.

So now, be ye landlubber or old salt, climb aboard for an exciting musical cruise. Distant ports of song and melody await us as we set sail for fun and adventure. Unlatch your sea chest, break out the ukulele. Tune your uke to the pitch of the bosun's pipe, and we'll weigh anchor and cast off to skim the waves and sail the ocean blue.

About The Author

Despite the lusty sentiments of the following songs, despite the hearty ho-heave-ho's of so many sea chanties and ballads of the briny deep, I must confess to preferring terre firma to sailing the ocean blue. To be sure I love the sea and all its traditions -- so long as I can love them on dry land.

It really shouldn't be this way. I grew up on Long Island Sound only a few miles from the Atlantic Ocean. As a teenager I crewed on a 30-foot sailboat, and while in the Marines logged in no small amount of sea duty on the South China Sea. My room as a boy was loaded with nautical memorabilia – fishing net curtains, seascape paintings, sailboat models, and a hat pointed fore and aft in the style of Admiral Horatio Hornblower. Even local girls in my hometown caught sea fever wearing port & starboard socks, one sock red and the other green, with pigtail ribbons similarly matched.

Summers were spent on Jones Beach where there was surf swimming in the ocean and living on Manhattan clam chowder with packets of oyster crackers. Nighttime brought sand dune beach parties, the crackle of driftwood fires, and the nearby crash of dark waves flecked by moonlight through scudding clouds. And there was singing and ukuleles – always singing and ukuleles!

Living now in the heart of the Finger Lakes region in upstate New York, I'm surrounded by lakes, inland waterways, and boats of all shapes and sizes. The old Erie Canal is minutes away and Lake Ontario not much further. Many times I have played for boat trips on these lakes and the Canal, yet despite all, I still like the feel of solid land under foot.

As I grew up and as musical interests developed, I discovered a special affection for songs of the sea. In high school I memorized poems (like Wallace Irwin's "A Nautical Experience") by setting them to music.

My imagination was and still is filled with visions of storms on the ocean, pirates flying their skull & crossbones, tales like Moby Dick, and, the narrative Scottish ballad of Sir Patrick Spens and his ill-omened doomed voyage for the king. I accompanied these reveries with ukulele and guitar, picking them out on the piano, often singing or whistling to myself when no instrument was at hand.

The sea songs in this collection are a significant sampling of those I treasure and am happy to share with you. With their vivid imagery and memorable melodies, I'm sure you'll find them just as rewarding as I have and every bit as enjoyable.

Prepare now for an exciting voyage. The tide is high, the sails are set, and the anchor's weighed. All aboard for unlimited fun and adventure and the satisfying fulfillment of making these songs your own.

COLUMBIA, THE GEM OF THE OCEAN

Ukulele tuning: gCEA

THOMAS à BECKETT, Sr.

COLUMBIA, THE GEM OF THE OCEAN

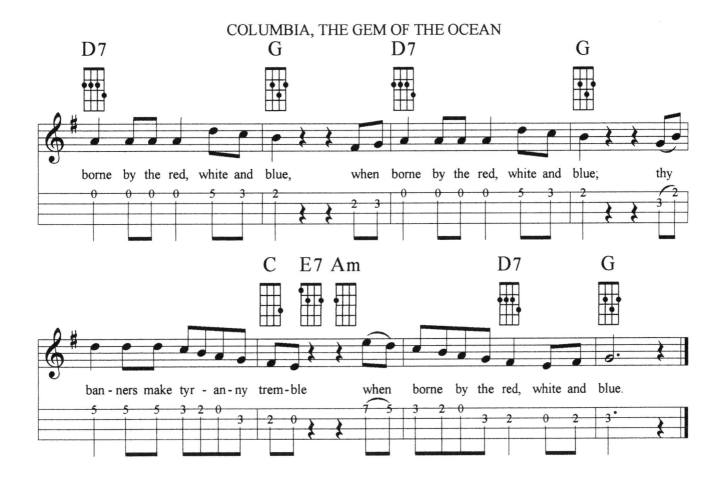

borne by the red, white and blue, when borne by the red, white and blue; thy

ban - ners make tyr - an-ny trem-ble when borne by the red, white and blue.

"Columbia" was an early nickname for the United States and was represented by a heroic woman often pictured with a sword or spear and draped in patriotic red, white and blue, stars and stripes.

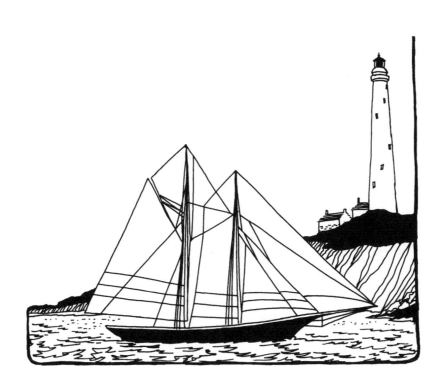

JACKY TAR

(A Hornpipe)

Ukulele tuning: gCEA

Traditional

LOCH LOMOND

Ukulele tuning: gCEA

Traditional Scottish

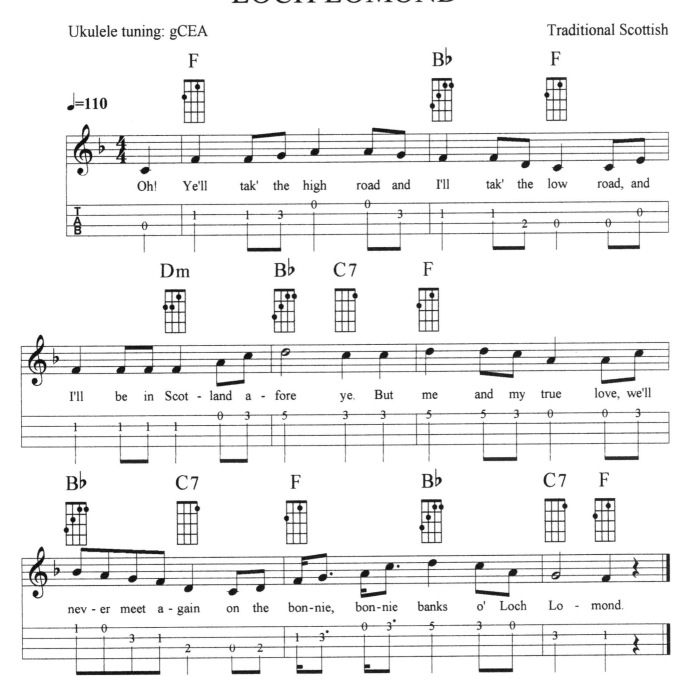

Situated on the boundary between the central lowlands of Scotland and the Scottish Highlands, Loch Lomond is the largest stretch of inland water in Great Britain. It measures 24 miles long and ranges from less than a mile to over file miles in width. Dotted with many islands, it is a popular tourist attraction rivaled in Scotland only by Loch Ness and its alleged sea monster.

MICHAEL, ROW THE BOAT

Ukulele tuning: gCEA

Traditional

2. The river is deep and the river is wide -- milk and honey on the other side. CHORUS
3. Jordan's river is chilly and cold -- chills the body but not the soul. CHORUS

MOONLIGHT BAY

Ukulele tuning: gCEA

EDWARD MADDEN   PERCY WENRICH

THE OCEANA ROLL

Ukulele tuning: gCEA

ROGER LEWIS

LUCIEN DENNI

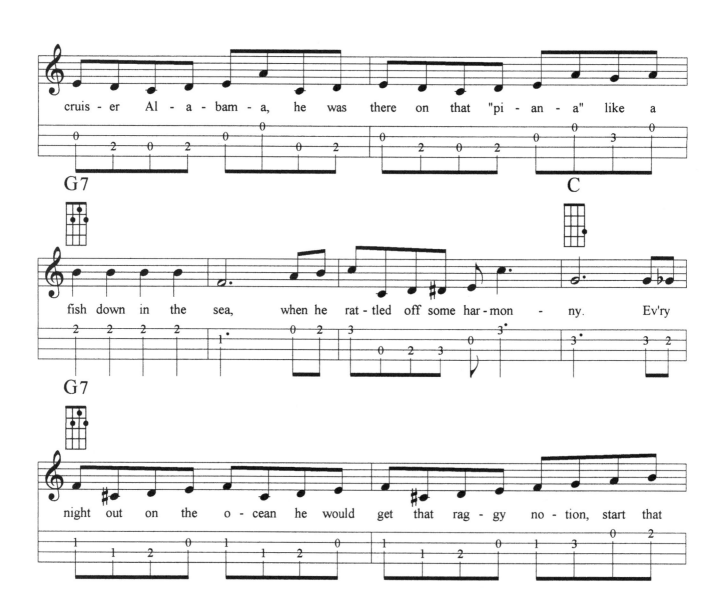

THE OCEANA ROLL

2. England or Spain, it was always the same,
   He'd be there at that "pi-an-a" on the cruiser Alabama.
   Ev'ry morning, noon and night,
   He'd keep it up with all his might.
   Ev'ry time he'd start a-playin'
   All the boys would start a-swayin'.
   Ev'ry one would keep a-saying, Don't you stop!"
   Sailors, take care! Oh, you sailors, beware!
   For Bill will play on 'till you drop.
   Chorus

ANCHORS AWEIGH

Ukulele tuning: gCEA

CHARLES A. ZIMMERMANN

Anchors aweigh. Said in preparation of getting underway, especially of a ship. An anchor that is aweigh is one that has just begun to put weight on the rope or chain by which it is being hauled up. Sailors were fond of adding "a" to words to make new ones, for example, 'astern', 'aboard;, ashore'. 'afloat', 'adrift', 'aground', etc.

BLOW THE MAN DOWN

Ukulele tuning: gCEA

Traditional

2. As I was walking down Paradise Street,
   'Way! Hey! Blow the man down!
   A frolicsome damsel I chanced for to meet,
   Give me some time to blow the man down.

3. She was round in the corner and bluff in the bow,
   So I took in all sail and cried, "Way enough now!"

4. She says then to me, "Will you stand me a treat?"
   "Delighted," says I, "for a charmer so sweet."

5. So I tailed her my flipper and took her in tow,
   And yardarm to yardarm, away we did go.

6. I bought her a dinner, two shillings in town,
   And trinkets and laces and bonnet and gown.

7. But I give you fair warning before we belay,
   Don't ever take heed of what pretty girls say.

BY THE BEAUTIFUL SEA

Ukulele tuning: gCEA

HAROLD R. ATTERIDGE   HARRY CARROLL

C

rich,   Ma   is   rich,   so   now   what   do   we   care?_____

F   **A7**

I   love   to   be   be - side   your   side,   be - side   the   sea,   be - side   the

D7   **G7**   **C**

sea - side_____   by   the   beau - ti - ful   sea._____

THE GREAT TITANIC

Ukulele tuning: gCEA

Traditional

THE GREAT TITANIC

Four days into her maiden voyage from Southampton to New York, the RMS Titanic struck an iceberg and sank in the north Atlantic on the morning of April 15, 1912. More than 1500 people lost their lives in what is considered the worst peacetime maritime disaster.

Yale University's famous a capella singing group, the Whiffenpoofs, has a delightful rendition of this song that they call "Jack, The Sailor.". Each verse is sung separately followed by a chorus. Then a verse and chorus are overlapped and sung simultaneously.

STRIKE UP THE BAND
(Here Comes A Sailor)

Ukulele tuning: gCEA

ANDREW B. STERLING

CHARLES B. WARD

ROW, ROW, ROW YOUR BOAT

Ukulele tuning: gCEA

Traditional

C

♩=110

Row, row, row your boat gen - tly down the stream,

G7   C

mer - ri - ly, mer - ri - ly, mer - ri - ly, mer - ri - ly, life is but a dream.

SANTA LUCIA

Ukulele tuning: gCEA

Neapolitan Boat Song

1.Now 'neath the sil-ver moon o-cean is glow-ing, o'er the calm bil - low

soft winds are blow-ing; Here balm - y breez-es blow, pure joys in - vite us,

and as we gent-ly row, all things de - light us. Hark, how the sail-or's cry

Chorus

joy - ous - ly ech-oes nigh: San - ta__ Lu - ci - a! San - ta Lu - ci - a.

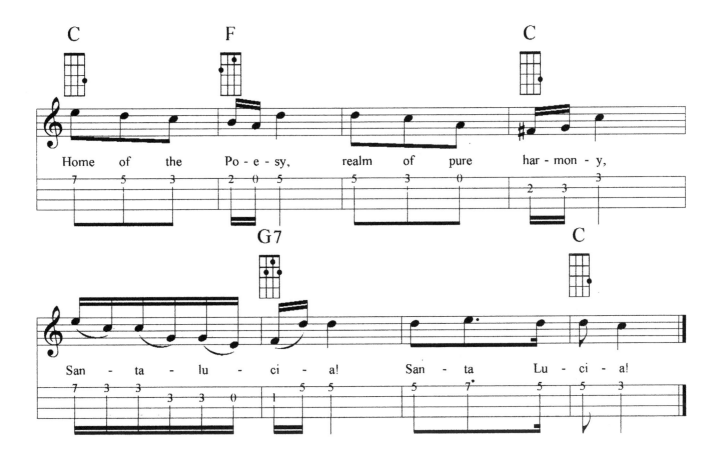

2. When o'er thy waters
   Light winds are playing,
   Thy spell can soothe us,
   All care allaying;
   To thee, sweet Napoli,
   What charms are given,
   Where smiles creation,
   Toil blest by heaven.
   Chorus

OVER THE WATERFALL

Ukulele tuning: gCEA

Traditional

REUBEN RANZO

Ukulele tuning: gCEA

Traditional Chantey

2. Ranzo was no sailor, Ranzo, boys, Ranzo,
   He shipped aboard a whaler, Ranzo, boys, yes Ranzo.

3. Ranzo joined the "Beauty" ... and didn't know his duty.

4. The skipper was a dandy ... and was too fond of brandy.

5. He called Ranzo a lubber ... and made him eat whale blubber.

6. Ranzo now is skipper ... of an old China Clipper.

Loose cannon. *An unpredictable person or thing. From the 17th century to the 19th century, wooden warships carried cannon as their primary offensive weapons. In order to avoid damage from their enormous recoil when fired they were mounted on rollers and secured with rope. A loose cannon was just what it sounds like, that is, a cannon that has become free of its restraints and was rolling dangerously about the deck.*

THE E-RI-E CANAL

Ukulele tuning: gCEA

Traditional

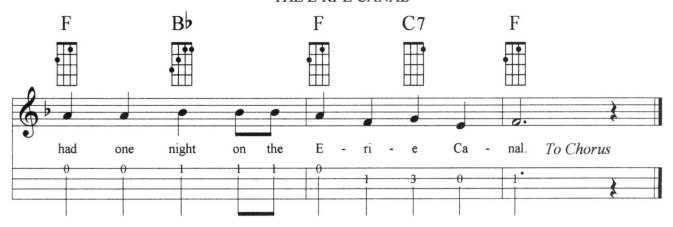

had one night on the E - ri - e Ca - nal. *To Chorus*

2. The captain, he come up on deck,
   A spyglass in his hand,
   But the fog it was so 'tarnel thick
   That he couldn't spy the land.
   Chorus

3. Two days out from Syracuse
   Our vessel struck a shoal,
   And we liked to foundered there
   On a chunk of Lakawanna coal.
   Chorus

4. We hollered to the captain
   On the towpath treading dirt;
   He jumped on board and stopped the leak
   With his old red flannel shirt.
   Chorus

5. Our cook, she was a grand old gal,
   She had a ragged dress;
   We hoisted her up on a pole
   As a signal of distress.
   Chorus

6. Our captain, he got married,
   Our cook she went to jail;
   And I'm the only sea cook's son
   Who's left to tell the tale.
   Chorus

A CAPITAL SHIP

Ukulele tuning: gCEA

From a poem by:
CHARLES E. CARRYL

Traditional

2. The bo'sun's mate was very sedate, yet fond of amusements, too.
   He played hop-scotch with the starboard watch, while the captain tickled the crew.
   The gunner we had was apparently mad, for he sat on the after rai-ai-ail,
   And fired salutes with the captain's boots in the teeth of a booming gale.
   Chorus

3. The captain sat on the commodore's hat, and dined in a royal way
   Off pickles and figs, and little roast pigs, and gunnery bread each day.
   The cook was Dutch and behaved as such, for the diet he served the crew-ew-ew,
   Was a couple of tons of hot-cross buns served up with sugar and glue.
   Chorus

4. Then we all fell ill as mariners will on a diet that's rough and crude,
   And we shivered and shook as we dipped the cook in a tub of his gluesome food.
   All nautical pride we cast aside, and we ran the vessel ashore-ore-ore
   On the Gulliby Isles, where the poopoo smiles, and the rubbily ubdugs roar.
   Chorus

5. Composed of sand was that favored land, and trimmed with cinnamon straws,
   And pink and blue was the pleasing hue of the tickle-toe-teaser's claws.
   We sat on the edge of a sandy ledge, and shot at the whistling bee-ee-ee,
   While the ring-tailed bats wore waterproof hats as they dipped in the shining sea.
   Chorus

6. On rugbug bark from dawn till dark we dined till we all had grown
   Uncommonly shrunk, when a Chinese junk came up from the Torrible Zone.
   She was chubby and square, but we didn't much care, so we cheerily put to sea-ee-ee,
   And we left all the crew of the junk to chew on the bark of the rugbug tree.
   Chorus

HULLABALOO BELAY

Ukulele tuning: gCEA

Traditional

2. A fresh young fellow named Shallo Brown, hullabaloo belay, hullabaloo below belay,
   He followed my mother all 'round the town, hullabaloo belay.

3. One day when father was on the crown, etc.
   My mother ran off with Shallo Brown, etc.

4. My father said to me,"Me, boy," etc.
   To which I quickly made reply, etc.

5. My father slowly pined away, etc.
   Because my mother came back the next day, etc.

O, WHEN THE TALL STACKS COMES TO TOWN!

Ukulele tuning: gCEA

SALLY LUKASIK

O, WHEN THE TALL STACKS COMES TO TOWN!

Sally Lukasik is the trumpet player with the Buffalo Ridge Jazz Band from Cincinnati, OH. The dynamic Dixieland group is led by long-time tenor banjo playing friend, Bob Adams. For more information about Tall Stacks see the notes for "The Glendy Burk" in this collection.

ON MIAMI SHORE

WILLIAM LE BARON

VICTOR JACOBI

On the gold - en sands of old Mi-
am - i shore
there I al - ways find a girl whom
I a - dore

How well I remember Arthur Godfrey -- relaxed, easygoing host of radio and TV shows -- singing this song while accompanying himself on a baritone ukulele. His radio show "Arthur Godfrey Time" ran from the 1940s to the 70s, a remarkable span of almost 30 years!

THE GLENDY BURK

Ukulele tuning: gCEA

STEPHEN C. FOSTER

Verse: 1. De Glen-dy Burk is a might-y fast boat, wida might-y fast cap-tain too, he
I can't stay here for dey work too hard, I'm bound to leave dis town, I'll

sits up dah on de hur-ri-cane roof, and he keeps his eye on de crew.
take my duds and tote 'em on/my back when de Glen-dy Burk comes down.

Chorus: Ho! for Lou'-si-an-a! I'm bound to leave dis town; I'll

take my duds and tote 'em on my back when de Glen-dy Burk comes down.

2. De Glendy Burk has a funny old crew
   And dey sing the boatman's song,
   Dey burn de pitch and de pine knot too,
   For to shove the boat along.
   De smoke goes up and de ingine roars,
   And de wheel goes round and round,
   So fare you well! I'll take a little ride
   When de Glendy Burk comes down.
   Chorus

3. I'll work all night in de wind and storm,
   I'll work all day in de rain,
   Till I find myself on de levy dock
   In New Orleans again.
   Dey make me mow in de hay field here
   And knock my head wid de flail,
   I'll go wha dey work wid de sugar and de cane
   And roll on de cotton bale.
   Chorus

4. My lady love is as pretty as a pink,
   I'll meet her on de way,
   I'll take her back to de sunny old south,
   And dah I'll make her stay.
   So don't you fret my honey dear,
   Oh! don't you fret Miss Brown,
   I'll take you back 'fore de middle of de week
   When the Glendy Burk comes down.
   Chorus

Every several years or so there's a festival in Cincinnati on the Ohio River called Tall Stacks. Paddle wheelers come from all over the Mississippi river to the Ohio, from as far north as Michigan and up from New Orleans and the deep south. I've had the good fortune to play for the event several times aboard the authentic steamboat, the "Belle of Louisville." The "Belle" is one of the larger ships like the "Delta Queen," the "Mississippi Queen" and the enormous "American Queen." But there are much smaller boats too, and the river and docks are dotted with a variety of many sizes.

In addition to the music that I was part of creating in the grand salon of the "Belle," there was the sound of steam calliopes echoing off the hills together with horn toots from ships coming and going. The calliope's shrill notes could be heard for miles, a traditionally way of alerting towns along the river of the boat's arrival. And for those special riverboats that provided entertainment, the calliope served to draw in the crowds and evoke the excited cries on shore of "Here comes the showboat!"

The "hurricane roof" mentioned in "The Glendy Burk" is the topmost deck of the boat, sometimes covered and sometimes not, providing passengers with an unobstructed view of passing scenery -- and the ship's captain with a good vantage point for checking up on the crew.

ROW, ROW, ROW

Ukulele tuning: gCEA

WILLIAM JEROME

JIMMIE V. MONACO

ROW, ROW, ROW

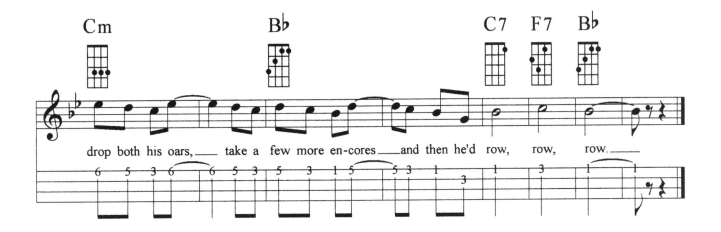

drop both his oars,___ take a few more en-cores___and then he'd row, row, row.___

2. Right in his boat he had a cute little seat,
And ev'ry kiss he stole from Flo was so sweet,
And he knew just how to row,
He was a rowing Romeo.
He knew an island where the trees were so grand,
He knew just where to land,
Then tales of love he'd tell to Flo,
Until it was time for then to go.
Chorus

SAILING DOWN THE CHESAPEAKE

Ukulele tuning: gCEA

JEAN HAVEZ

GEORGE BOTSFORD

SAILING DOWN THE CHESAPEAKE

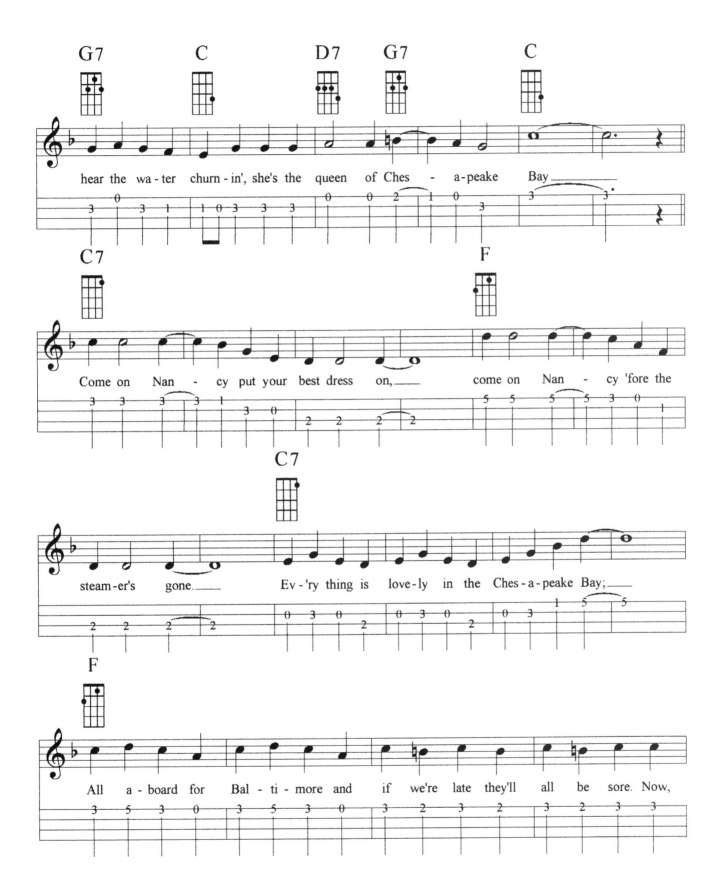

BANKS OF THE OHIO

Ukulele tuning: gCEA

Traditional

2. And only say that you'll be mine, and in no other arms entwine,
   Down beside where the waters flow, down by the banks of the O-hi-o.

3. I asked your mother for you, dear, and she said you were too young.
   But only say that you'll be mine, happiness in my home you'll find.

SAILOR'S HORNPIPE

Ukulele tuning: gCEA

Traditional

BELL-BOTTOM TROUSERS

Ukulele tuning: gCEA

Traditional

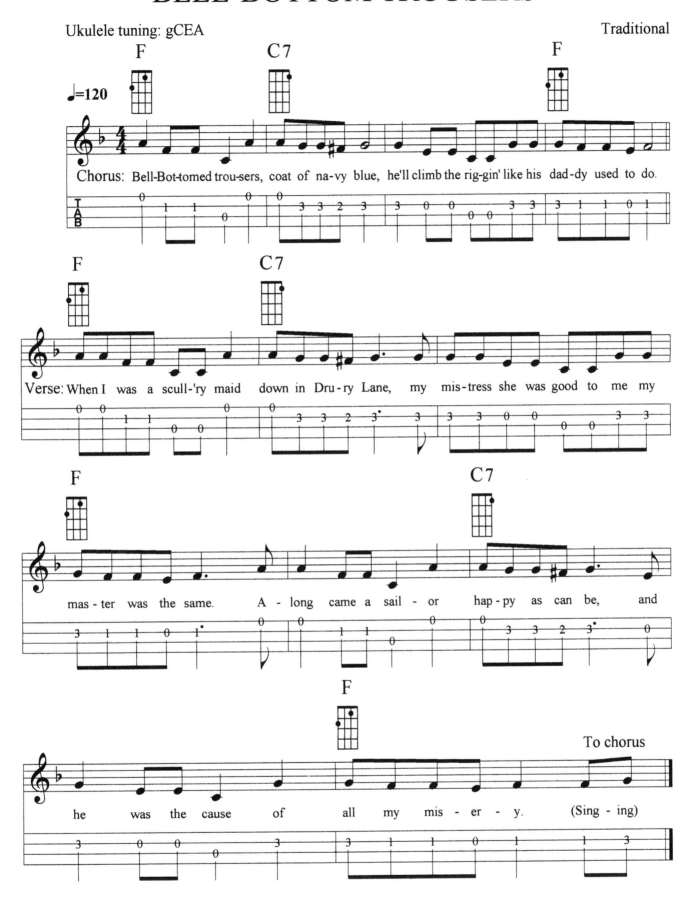

SAILING, SAILING

Ukulele tuning: gCEA

GODFREY MARKS

BOBBY SHAFTO

Ukulele tuning: gCEA

Traditional English

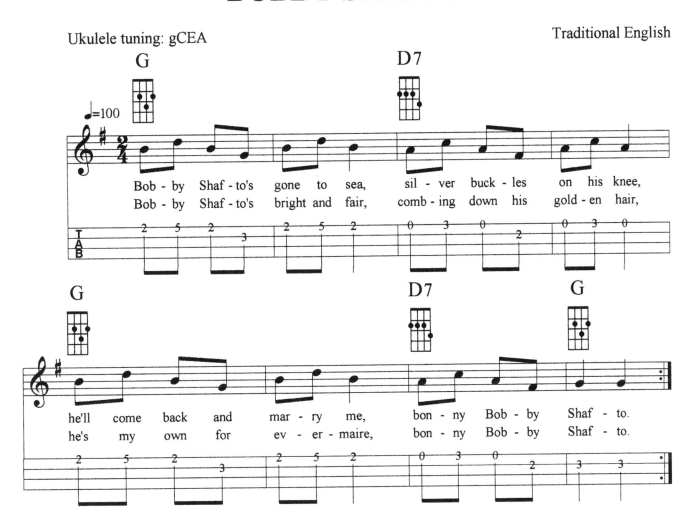

Bob - by Shaf - to's gone to sea, sil - ver buck - les on his knee,
Bob - by Shaf - to's bright and fair, comb - ing down his gold - en hair,

he'll come back and mar - ry me, bon - ny Bob - by Shaf - to.
he's my own for ev - er - maire, bon - ny Bob - by Shaf - to.

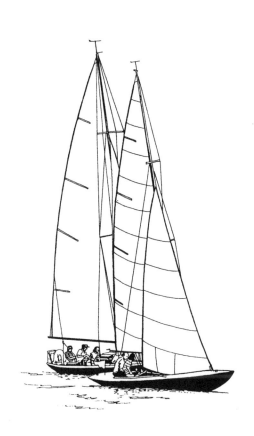

SHALL WE GATHER AT THE RIVER?

Ukulele tuning: gCEA

ROBERT LOWRY

2. On the margin of the river, washing up its silver spray,
   We will talk and worship ever, all the happy golden day.
   REFRAIN

3. Ere we reach the shining river, lay we every burden down,
   Grace our spirits will deliver, and provide a robe and crown.
   REFRAIN

4. At the smiling of the river, mirror of the Savior's face,
   Saints, whom death will never sever, lift their songs of saving grace.
   REFRAIN

5. Soon we'll reach the silver river, soon our pilgrimage will cease,
   Soon our happy hearts will quiver, with the melody of peace.
   REFRAIN

WAITIN' FOR THE ROBERT E. LEE

Ukulele tuning: gCEA

L.WOLFE GILBERT

LEWIS F. MUIR

Lyrics:

1.Way down on the lev - ee, in old Al - a - bam_ y, there's dad - dy and mam - my, there's E - phra'm and Sam - my; on a moon - light night you can find_ them all; while they are wait - in', the ban-jos are syn - co - pa-tin'. What's that they're say - in'? Oh, what's that they're say - in'? The

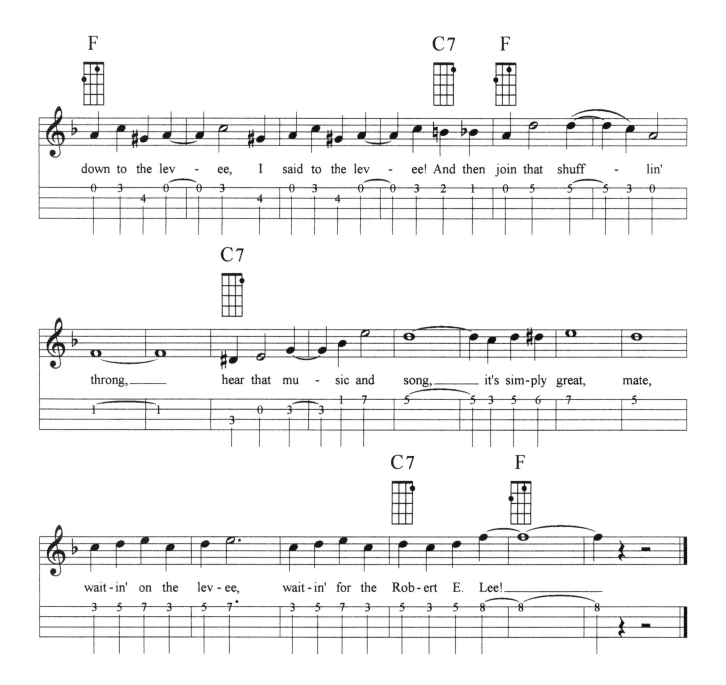

2. The whistles are blowin', the smokestacks are showin',
   The ropes they are throwin',   Excuse me, I'm goin'
   To the place where all is harmonious,
   Even the preacher, they say is the dancing teacher.
   Have you been down there? Say, were you aroun' there?
   If you ever go there, you'll always be found there.
   Why, "doggone", here comes my baby
   On the good old ship Robert E. Lee.

SHENANDOAH

Originally a work song for hoisting anchor and sails, this sea chanty reached dry land, and like like many folk songs, eventually acquired a number of lyric variations. The name "Shenandoah" appealed to Civil War soldiers who may have associated it with a home west of the Missouri River in Shenandoah, Iowa, or one in the Shenandoah Valley, or nearby the Shenandoah River that joined the Potomac River at Harpers Ferry, site of John Brown's famous raid.

Ukulele tuning: gCEA

Traditional

SHENANDOAH -- the rich, fertile Valley of Virginia, the so-called granary and bread basket of the Confederate army. In a Federal scorched-earth policy, the Valley was devastated by the Army of the Shenandoah under the command of General "Little Phil" Sheridan. Although small in stature, measuring just five foot four inches, a foot shorter than Abraham Lincoln, Sheridan was a fierce warrior and brilliant commander, a favorite of General Ulysses S. Grant.

DOWN BY THE RIVERSIDE

Ukulele tuning: gCEA

Traditional

2. Gonna lay down my sword and shield
   Down by the riverside (3x)
   Gonna lay down my sword and shield
   Down by the riverside (2x)
   CHORUS

3. Gonna try on my long white robe, etc.

4. Gonna try on my starry crown, etc.

4. Gonna put on my golden shoes, etc.

THE IRISH ROVER

Ukulele tuning: gCEA

Traditional

Verse 1. In the year of our Lord, eigh-teen hun-dred and six, we set sail from the quay of Cork, we were

sail - ing a - way with a car - go of bricks for the grand Cit - y Hall in New York. We'd an

el - e - gant craft, it was rigged fore and aft, and how the trade winds drove her. She had

twen - ty four masts and she stood sev - 'ral blasts, and they called her the I - rish Rov - er.

Verse 2.
We had one million bags of the best Sligo rags,
We had two million barrels of bone,
We had three million bales of old nanny goats' tails,
We had four million barrels of stone.
We had five million hogs and six million dogs,
And seven million barrels of porter,
We had eight million sides of old horses' hides,
In the hold of the Irish Rover.

Verse 3.
There was Barney McGee from the banks of the Lee,
There was Hogan from County Tyrone,
There was Johnny McGirk, who was scared stiff of work,
And a lad from Westmeath called Malone.
There was Slugger O'Toole, who was drunk as a rule,
There was fighting Jack Gooley from Dover,
And a sea-going man from the banks of the Bann
Was skipper of the Irish Rover.

Verse 4.
We had sailed seven years when the mizzen broke out,
And the ship lost its way in the fog,
And that whale of a crew was reduced down to two,
Just myself and the captain's old dog,.
Then the ship struck a rock, O Lord, what a shock!
The bulhead was turned right over,
Turned upside down, and the poor dog was drowned,
I'm the last of the Irish Rover.

THE SHIP THAT NEVER RETURNED

HENRY CLAY WORK

Verse: 1.On a sum - mer's day while the waves were rip - pling with a
sweet fare - wells, there were lov - ing sig - nals, while a

qui - et and a gen - tle breeze;_____ A _____ ship set sail with a
form ___ was ___ yet dis - cerned,_____ tho they knew it not, 'twas a

car - go lad - den for a port be - yond the sea._____ There were
sol - em part - ing for the ship, she never re - turned._____ Did she

Chorus: ev - er re - turn? No, she nev - er re - turned, and her fate is still un -

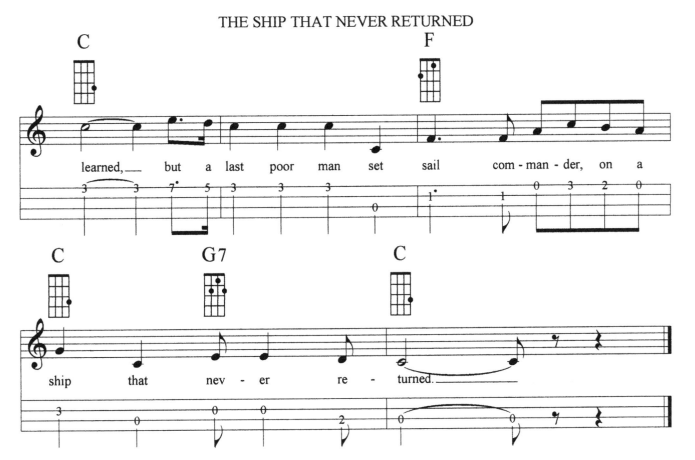

learned,___ but a last poor man set sail com-man-der, on a

ship that nev - er re - turned.____

2. Said a feeble lad to his anxious mother,
   "I must cross the wide, wide sea,
   For they say, perchance, in a foreign climate
   There is health and strength for me.
   'Twas a gleam of hope in a maze of danger,
   And her heart for her youngest yearned;
   Yet she sent him forth with a smile and blessing
   On the ship that never returned. *Chorus*

3. "Only one more trip," said a gallant seaman,
   As he kissed his weeping wife;
   "Only one more bag of golden treasure,
   And will last us all through life.
   Then I'll spend my days in a cozy cottage,
   And enjoy the rest I've earned;"
   But alas, poor man! for he sailed commander
   On the ship that never returned. *Chorus*

Best known for his songs from the Civil War period, "Marching Through Georgia" and "Kingdon Coming," Henry Clay Work is also remembered for the minstrel show favorite "Wake Nicodemus" and "My Grandfather's Clock," which gave rise to the name of that tall timepiece. The popular folk group "Kingston Trio" did a take-off on "The Ship That Never Returned" with their parody song "M.T.A." about a man named Charlie destined to ride forever on the Boston subway. With minor variations the melody is also found in the folk song of railroad disater, "The Wreck Of The Old 97."

THE WATER IS WIDE

Ukulele tuning: gCEA

Traditional English

1.The wa-ter is wide,_____ I can-not get o'er,_____ nei-ther do

I_____ have wings to___ fly;_____ build me a___

boat_____ that will car - ry___ two,_____ and both will

row,_____ my love and I._____

2. A ship there is, and she sails the sea.
   She's loaded deep, as deep can be.
   But not so deep as the love I'm in,
   I know not if I sink or swim.

3. I leaned my back against an oak tree
   Thinking it was a trusty tree,
   But first it bent and then it broke,
   So did my love prove false to me.

4. Oh, love be handsome and love be kind,
   Gay as a jewel when first it is new,
   But loves grows old and waxes cold,
   And fades away like the morning dew.

5. When cockle shells turn silver bells,
   Then will my love come back to me;
   When roses bloom in winter's gloom,
   Then will my love return to me.

There are many variations of this lovely Scotch-English ballad. One such adaptation is the Irish "Carrickfergus" with lyrics that begin:

"I wish I was in Carrickfergus, only for nights in Ballygran.
I would swim over the deepest ocean, the deepest ocean my love to find.
But the sea is wide and I cannot swim over, and neither have I wings to fly.
If I could find me a handsome boatman to ferry me over to my love and die..."

A wide berth. *A goodly distance, originally a nautical term, dating back to the heyday of sail.*

THE EDDYSTONE LIGHT

Ukulele tuning: gCEA

Traditional

1.My fa-ther was the keep-er of the Ed-dy-stone Light and he slept with a mer-maid one fine night. And from this un - ion there came three, a por - gy, and a por - poise, and the oth - er was me.

Chorus

Yo, ho, ho, the wind blows free, oh, for a life on the roll - ing sea.

2. One fine night while a-trimmin' o' the glim
   And a-singing a verse from the evening hymn.
   A voice off starboard shouted, "Ahoy!"
   And there was my mother a-sitting on a buoy.
   Chorus

3. "What has become of my children three?"
   My mother then she asked of me.
   "One was exhibited as a talking fish
   And the other was served in a chafffing dish."
   Chorus

4. The phosphorus gleamed in her seaweed hair,
   I looked again and my mother wasn't there.
   A voice came echoing out of the night,
   "Your father was the keeper of the Eddystone Light.!"
   Chorus

NOTE: The Eddystone Light was a real lighthouse, located on the Eddystone Reef 14 miles from Plymouth off the storm-lashed coast of Cornwall. The dangerous reef was mostly submerged with only a small portion visible on which a succession of five lighthouses was built. After numerous ships floundered on the reef, the first Eddystone was erected in 1699, only to be destroyed four years later in one of the worst hurricanes ever recorded. It was rebuilt in 1803 and three times after that, the last constructed in 1882 -- a history spanning two centuries.

SLOOP JOHN B

Ukulele tuning: gCEA

Bahama Islands

With a
Calypso beat

♩=140

Verse: 1.We come on___ the Sloop John B, my grand - fath-er and me, 'round Nas - sau Town we___ did roam.___ Drink-ing all night,___ got in-to a fight,___ I feel so break-up___ I wan-na go___

CHORUS: (Same melody as verse.)
So, hoist up the John B sails,
See how the mainsail sets,
Send for the captain ashore, let me go home.
Let me go home, I wanna go home,
I feel so break-up, I want to go home.

VERSE:
2. The first mate he got drunk,
   Break up the people's trunk,
   Constable come aboard and take him away.
   Mr. Johnstone, why don't you let me alone?
   I feel so break-up, I wanna go home.
   Chorus

3. The poor cook he got the fits,
   Throw away all o' my grits,
   Captain's pig done eat up all of the corn.
   Let me go home, I wanna go home,
   This is the worst trip since I was born.
   Chorus

ALL FOR ME GROG

Ukulele tuning: gCEA

Traditional

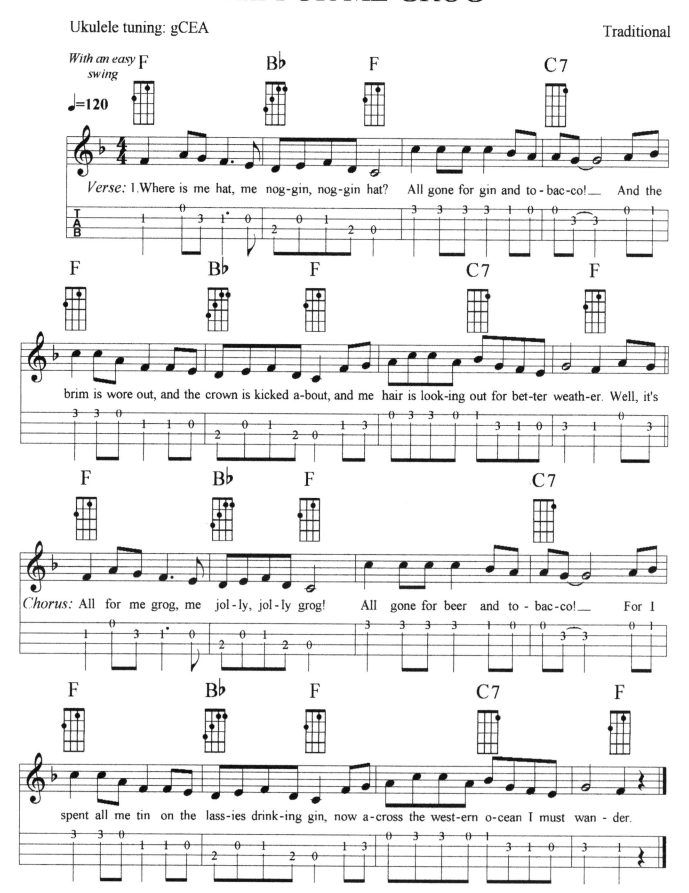

Verse: 1.Where is me hat, me nog-gin, nog-gin hat? All gone for gin and to-bac-co!__ And the

brim is wore out, and the crown is kicked a-bout, and me hair is look-ing out for bet-ter weath-er. Well, it's

Chorus: All for me grog, me jol-ly, jol-ly grog! All gone for beer and to-bac-co!__ For I

spent all me tin on the lass-ies drink-ing gin, now a-cross the west-ern o-cean I must wan - der.

2. Where is me shirt, me noggin, noggin shirt?
   All gone for gin and tobacco!
   And the sleevs are worn out,
   And the collar's knocked about,
   And the tails is looking out for better weather.
   Chorus

3. Where are me boots, me noggin, noggin boots?
   All gone for gin and tobacco!
   And the soles are worn out,
   And the heels are kicked about,
   And me toes are looking out for better weather.
   Chorus

4. Where are me pants, me noggin, noggin pants?
   All gone for gin and tobacco!
   And the cuffs are worn out,
   And the fly is knocked about,
   And me arse is looking out for better weather.
   Chorus

5. I'm sick to my head, and I haven't been to bed,
   Since I first came ashore with all me plunder;
   I see centipedes and snakes,
   And I'm full of pains and aches,
   And I guess it's time to shove off over yonder.
   Chorus

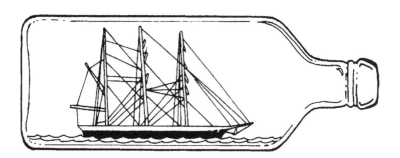

SKYE BOAT SONG

Ukulele tuning: gCEA

Traditional Scottish

2. Tho the waves leap, soft shall ye sleep,
   Ocean's a royal bed;
   Rocked in the deep, Flora* will keep
   Watch by your weary head.
       Chorus

3. Many's the lad fought on that day,
   Well claymore** could wield;
   When night came, silently lay
   Dead on Culloden's field.
       Chorus

4. Burn'd are our homes, exile and death
   Scatter'd our loyal men;
   Yet, e'er the sword cool in the sheath,
   Charlie will come again.
       Chorus

* Flora -- Flora MacDonald, disguised Prince Charles as her maidservant thereby
  aiding his escape.

** Claymore -- A broad doubled-edged sword favored by Scottish Highlanders.

Note: The Battle of Culloden Moors in 1756 pitted Prince Charles Edward Stuart ("Bonnie Prince Charlie") and his clans of Highlanders against the Duke of Cumberland in an attempt to regain the British throne and re-seat the House of Stuart. Charles was defeated and escaped to the Isle of Skye, situated in the Inner Hebrides off the west coast of Scotland.

THE MERMAID

Uukulele tuning: gCEA

Traditional

THE MERMAID

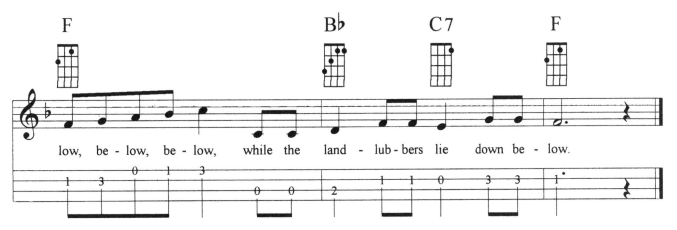

low, be - low, be - low,   while the   land - lub - bers lie   down be - low.

2. Then up spoke the captain of our gallant ship.
   And a right-spoken man was he,
   "I married me a wife in old Salem town,
   And tonight she a widow will be."
   Chorus

3. Then up spoke the cook of our gallant ship,
   And a right good cookie was he,
   "I care more for my pots and my pans
   Then I do for the bottom of the sea."
   Chorus

4. Then up spoke the cabin boy of our gallant ship,
   And a dirty little rat was he.
   "There's nary a soul in old Salem town
   Who cares anything about me."
   Chorus

5. Then three times around went our gallant ship,
   And three times around went she.
   Three times around went our gallant ship,
   And she sank to the bottom of the sea.
   Chorus

Mariners are a superstitious lot, and the sight of a mermaid was considered to be an ill omen. And so it was for this doomed ship after spotting one of Neptune's daughters combing her seaweed hair and preening herself in a looking glass.

Between the Devil and the deep blue sea. *In difficulty, faced with two alternatives.*

WHEN I WAS A LAD

(From the Operetta "H.M.S. Pinafore")

W.S. GILBERT   Ukulele tuning: gCEA   SIR ARTHUR SULLIVAN

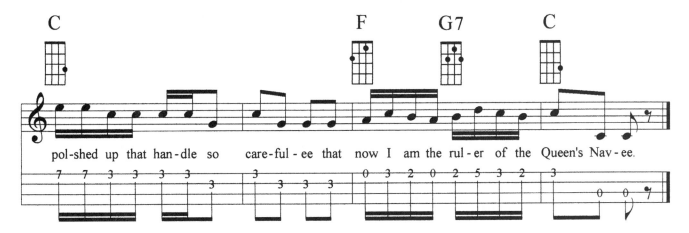

pol-shed up that han-dle so care-ful-ee that now I am the rul-er of the Queen's Nav-ee.

2. As office boy I made such a mark
   That they gave me the post of a junior clerk.
   I served the writs with a smile so bland,
   And copied all the letters in a big round hand.
   {I copied all the letters in a hand so free,
   That now I am the ruler of the Queen's Navee} 2X

3. In serving writs I made such a name
   That an articled clerk I soon became;
   I wore clean collars and a bran' new suit
   For the pass examination at the Institute.
   {That pass examination did so well for me
   That now I am the ruler of the Queen's Navee.} 2X

4. Of legal knowledge I acquired such a grip
   That they took me into the partnership,
   And that junior partnership, I ween,
   Was the only ship that I had ever seen.
   {But that kind of ship so suited me
   That now I am the ruler of the Queen's Navee.} 2X

5. I grew so rich that I was sent
   By a pocket borough into Parliament.
   I always voted at my party's call,
   And I never thought of thinking for myself at all.
   {I thought so little, they rewarded me,
   By making me the ruler of the Queen's Navee.} 2X

6. Now landsmen all, whoever you may be,
   If you want to rise to the top of the tree,
   If your soul isn't fettered to an office stool,
   Be careful to be guided by this golden rule:
   {Stick close to your desks and never go to sea,
   And you all may be rulers of the Queen's Navee.} 2X

CAPE COD GIRLS

Ukulele tuning: gCEA

Traditional

2. Cape Cod girls are very fine girls,
   Heave away! Heave a-way!
   With codfish balls they comb their curls,
   We are bound for California.
   Chorus

3. Cape Cod boys they have no sleds,
   Heave a-way! Heave a-way!
   They slide down hills on codfish heads,
   We are bound for California.
   Chorus

4. Cape Cod cats they have no tails,
   Heave a-way! Heave a-way!
   They lost them all in nor'east gales,
   We are bound for Califnornia.
   Chorus

5. Cape Cod doctors have no pills,
   Heave away! Heave a-way!
   They give their patients codfish gills,
   We are bound for California.
   Chorus

GOLDEN VANITY

Ukulele tuning: gCEA

Traditional

♩=120

1.There once was a ship sailed up - on the Low-land sea, and the name of that ship was the

"Gold - en Van - i - ty," and we feared she would be tak - en by the Span - ish en - e - my as she

sailed up - on the Low - land, Low - land, Low, as she sailed up - on the Low - land sea,

2. Then up spoke our cabin boy, and bodly outspoke he,
    And he said to the captain, "What will you give to me,
    If I swim alonside of the Spanish enemy
    And sink her in the Lowland, Lowland, Low,
    And sink her in the Lowland sea?"

3. "Oh, I will give you silver, and I will give you gold,
   And my own fair daughter your bonny brideshall be,
   If you'll swim alongside of the Spanish enemy
   And sink her in the Lowland, Lowland, Low,
   And sink her in the Lowland sea."

4. Then the boy he made him ready, and overboard sprang he,
   And he swam alongside of the Spanish enemy,
   And with his brace and auger in her side he bored holes three,
   And he sank her in the Lowland, Lowland, Low,
   And he sank her in the Lowland sea.

5. Then quickly he swam back to the cheering of the crew,
   But the captain would not heed him, for his promise he did rue,
   And he scorned his poor entreatings when loudly he did sue,
   And left him in the Lowland, Lowland, Low,
   And left him in the Lowland sea.

6. Then roundabout he turned, and he swam to the port side,
   And up unto his messmates full bitterly he cried,
   "Oh, messmates, draw me up for I'm drifting with the tide,
   And I'm sinking in the Lowland, Lowland, Low,
   And I'm sinking in the Lowland sea."

7. Then his messmates drew him up, but on the deck he died,
   And they stitched him in his hammock, which was so fair and wide,
   And they lowered him overboard, and he drifted with the tide,
   And he sank in the Lowland, Lowland, Low,
   And he sank in the Lowland sea.

HIGH BARBARY

Ukulele tuning: gCEA

Traditional

1.There were two ships from old Eng-land came. Blow high, blow low, and so sailed we. One was the "Prince of Lu-ther" and the oth-er "Prince of Wales," sail-ing down a-long the coast of High Bar-ba-ry.

2. "Aloft there, aloft!" our jolly boatswain cried,
   Blow high, blow low, and so sailed we;
   "Look ahead, look astern, look a-weather, look alee,"
   Sailing down along the coast of High Barbary.

3. "There's naught upon the stern, there's naught upon the lee,"
   Blow high, blow low, and so sailed we;
   "But there's a ship to windward and a lofty ship she be,"
   Sailing down along the coast of High Barbary.

4. "Now are you a pirate of a man-o'-war?" cried we;
   "We are not a pirate but a man-o'-war," cried she.

5. "Lower your topsail and bring your vessel to;
   For we have some letters to be sent home by you."

6. "We'll lower our topsails and bring our vessel to;
   But only in a harbor and alongside of you."

7. 'Twas broadside to broadside, a long time we lay;
   Until the "Prince Of Luther" shot the pirate's masts away.

8. "Have mercy, oh have mercy!" the lusty pirates cried;
   But the mercy that we gave them was to sink them in the tide.

9. Oh, it was a cruel sight and it grieved us all full sore;
   To see them all a-drowning as they tried to swim ashore.

~oOo~

There's a certain romance connected with pirates and piracy. The image of black flags with skull and crossbones, swashbuckling buccaneers swinging on ropes, flashing cutlasses, knives clentched in teeth, long-barreled pistols, golden earrings, peglegs -- it's all there for the taking in novels, movies, and sea chanties like "High Barbary." The reality, however, is quite different. Piracy was brutal -- slaughter, pillage and plunder. Cargo was looted. Ships were captured, destroyed, or burned to the waterline.

The Barbary coast of northern Africa along the Mediterranean Sea was notorious for piracy. It still is, and piracy continues today off the coast of Somali and the Gulf of Aden. Vessels are captured, hostages taken, ransoms demanded. Legendary figures like Blackbeard, Henry Morgan, and Grace O'Malley ("The Pirate Queen") are replaced by modern pirates with automatic weapons and sophisticated electronic gear.

But by way of departure and a lighthearted escape from these perils of the high seas, you'll be sure to find merry moments of enjoyment with Gilbert & Sullivan's delightful operetta "The Pirates Of Penzance."

MY BONNIE LIES OVER THE OCEAN

Ukulele tuning: gCEA

Traditional

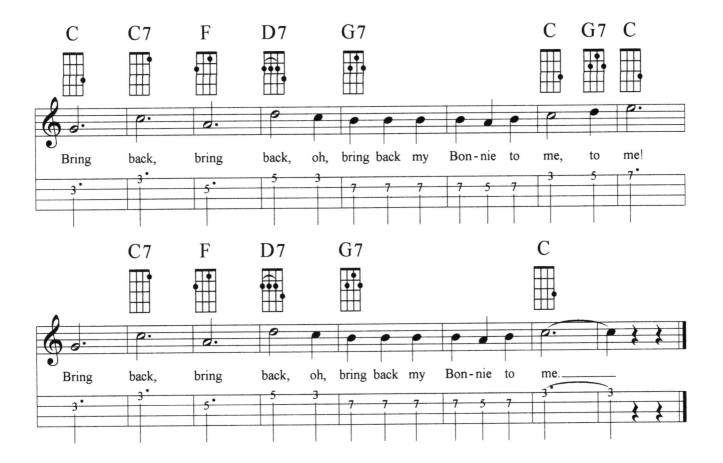

Bring back, bring back, oh, bring back my Bon-nie to me, to me!

Bring back, bring back, oh, bring back my Bon-nie to me.

Verse 2. Oh, blow the winds over the ocean,
Oh, blow the winds over the sea,
Oh, blow the winds over the ocean,
And bring back my Bonnie to me.

SOUTH AUSTRALIA

Ukulele tuning: gCEA

Traditional

2. As I went out one morning fair,
   Heave away, haul away,
   There I met Miss Nancy Blair,
   We're bound for South Australia.
   Chorus

3. I danced her up, I danced her down,
   Heave away, haul away,
   I danced her round and round the town,
   We're bound for South Australia.
   Chorus

4. There ain't but one thing grieves my mind,
   Heave away, haul away,
   To leave Miss Nancy Blair behind,
   We're bound for South Australia.
   Chorus

5. When we lollop around Cape Horn,
   Heave away, haul away,
   You'll wish to God you'd never be born,
   We're bound for South Australia.
   Chorus

SWEET AND LOW

Ukulele tuning: gCEA

ALFRED, LORD TENNYSON

SIR JOSEPH BARNBY

1.Sweet and low, sweet and low, wind of the west - ern sea;

low, low, breathe and blow, wind of the west - ern sea;

o - ver the roll - ing wa - ters go, come from the dy - ing moon and blow,

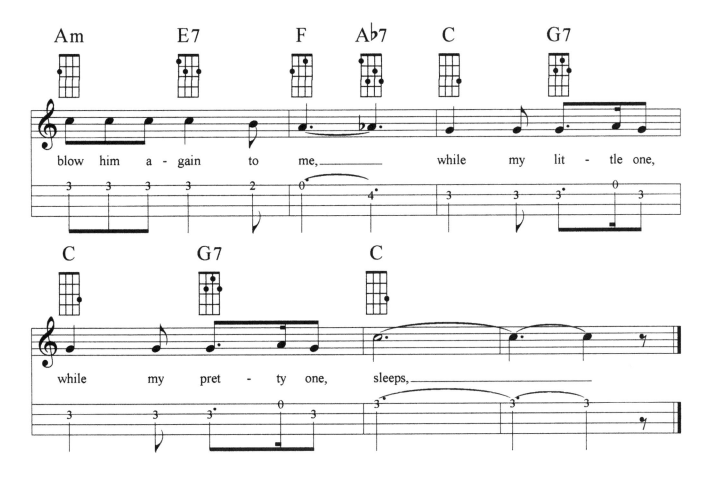

blow him a - gain to me,_____ while my lit - tle one, while my pret - ty one, sleeps,_____

2. Sleep and rest,
   Sleep and rest,
   Father will come to thee soon;
   Rest, rest on
   Mother's breast,
   Father will come to thee soon;
   Father will come to his babe in the nest,
   Silver sails all out of the west,
   Under the silver moon,
   Sleep, my little one,
   Sleep, my pretty one,
   Sleep.

One of the best loved comic operas of all times, Gilbert & Sullivan's *HMS Pinafore* has delighted audiences for over one hundred years with its cast of zaney characters and rollicking musical score. First produced in London in 1878, it was followed a year later in New York City by another comic opera also with the hint of a seafaring theme, the *Pirates of Penzance.*

CAPTAIN OF THE PINAFORE
(My Gallant Crew)

Ukulele tuning: gCEA

W.S. GILBERT

SIR ARTHUR SULLIVAN

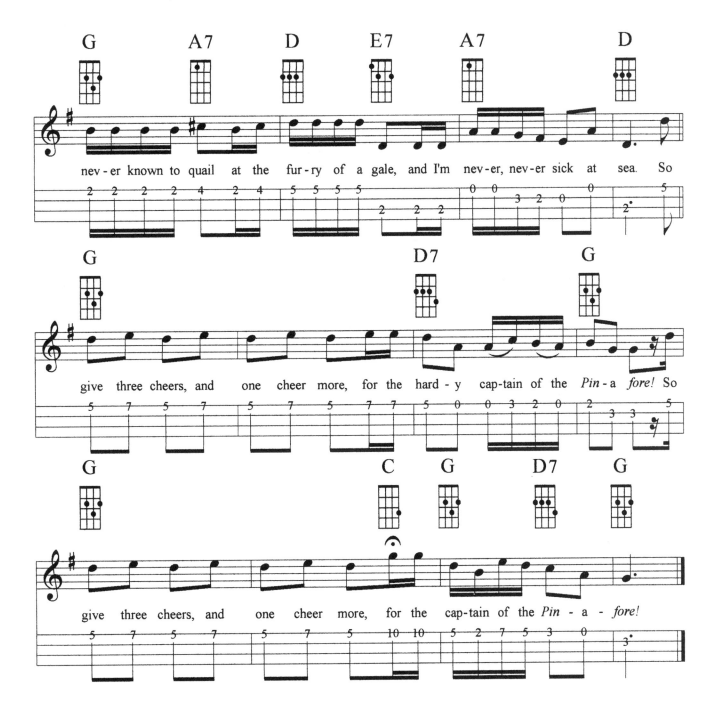

FROM THE CAPTAIN TO THE CREW:
2. I do my best to satisfy you all --
   (And with you we're quite content.)
   You're exceedingly polite, and I think it only right
   To return the compliment.
   Bad language or abuse, I never, never use,
   Whatever the emergency;
   Though "bother it" I may -- occasionally say,
   I never use a big, big D___.
        Then give three cheers ... etc.

DE BOATMEN'S DANCE

Ukulele tuning: gCEA

DAN D. EMMIT

DE BOATMEN'S DANCE

dance de boat-men dance, O dance de boat-men dance, O

dance all night till broad day-light, an go home wid de gals in de morn-ing.

2. De oyster boat should keep to de shore,
   De fishin' boat should venture more,
   De schooner sails before the wind,
   De steamboat leaves a streak behind.
      O dance, boatmen, dance ... etc.

3. When you go to de boatmen's ball,
     Dance wid my wife, or don't dance at all;
   Sky blue jacket an tarpaulin hat,
   Look out my boys for the nine tail cat.
      O dance, boatmen, dance ... etc.

4. De boatman is a thrifty man,
   Dars none can do as the boatman can;
   I neber see a putty gal in my life
   But dat she was a boatman's wife.
      O dance, boatmen, dance ... etc.

5. When de boatman blows his horn,
     Look out old man your hog is gone;
   He cotch my sheep, he cotch my shoat,
   Den put em in a bag and toat em to do boat.
      O dance, boatmen, dance ...

Dan Emmett and the group he formed in 1843, the Virginia Minsrels, are credited with establishing the format for minstrel shows that remained popular for almost 100 years. Consisting of four members, all in blackface, Emmett's troupe performed on fiddle, banjo, tambourine and bones. In addition to "De Boatmen's Dance," Emmett is best known for composing the song "Dixie," said to be a favorite of President Abraham Lincoln, despite his northern sympathies.

I'VE BEEN FLOATING DOWN
THE OLD GREEN RIVER

BERT KALMER   Ukulele tuning: gCEA   JOE COOPER

Husbands out on the town who come staggering home in the wee hours
can certainly tell their wives some whoppers, but this one tops them all!

GREENLAND FISHERIES

Ukulele tuning: gCEA

Traditional

Note: Whaling was prevalent not only in the 1800s but prior, and to some extent exists today.
Not only was whaling a major industry in New England and England itself, but throughout the
English speaking world. The perils of this occupation were frequent -- violent storms at sea and
the dangerous harpooning of the whale. Even when a mamouth whale was "struck" the harpooning
boat could be towed on a furious "Nantucket sleigh ride." Along with this well-known song of the
sea, the sense of whaling is captured to perfection in Herman Melville's 1851 novel "Moby-Dick."

2. Our captain stood on the quarterdeck
   With a spyglass in his hand,
   "There's a whale, there's a whale, there's a whalefish," he cried,
   And she blows at every span, brave boys,
   And she blows at every span."

3. The boats were launched with the men on board,
   With the whalefish well in view,
   And well prepared were our jolly fishermen
   For to strike when the whalefish blew, brave boys,
   For to strike when the whalefish blew.

4. Then the whalefish struck, and the line was played out,
   But he gave such a flounder with his tail,
   That the boat capsized and five men were lost,
   And we never did catch that whale, brave boys,
   And we never did catch that whale.

5. The loss of that whalefish did grieve our hearts,
   It did grieve our hearts full score,
   But, oh!, the loss of our five shipmates
   Did grieve us ten times more, brave boys,
   Did grieve us ten times more.

6. "Up anchor! Up anchor!" our captain cried,
   "Let us leave this cold country,
   With the storms and the snow, where the whalefishes blow,
   And the daylight's seldom seen, brave boys,
   Where the daylight's seldom seen."

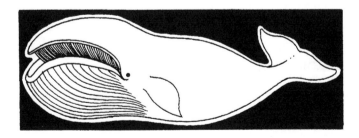

BLOW, YE WINDS, IN THE MORNING

Ukulele tuning: gCEA

TRADITIONAL

2. They send you to New Bedford, that famous whaling port,
And give you to some land-sharks to board and fit you out, singing:
Chorus

3. They tell you of the clipper ships a-running in and out,
And say you'll take 500 sperm before you're six months out, singing:
Chorus

4. It's now we're out to sea, my boys, the wind comes out to blow,
One half the watch is sick on deck, the other half below, singing:
Chorus

5. The skipper's on the quarterdeck, a-squinting at the sails,
When up aloft the lookout sights a school of whales, singing:
Chorus

6. "Now clear away the boats, my boys, and after him we'll travel,
But if you get too near his fluke, he'll kick you like the devil," singing:
Chorus

7. And now we've got him turned up, we tow him alongside,
We over with our blubber-hooks and rob him of his hide, singing:
Chorus

8. But now that our old ship is full and we don't give a damn,
We'll bend on all our stu'nsails and sail for Yankee land, singing:
Chorus

9. When we get home, our ship made fast, and we get through our sailing,
A winding glass around we'll pass and damn this blubber whaling, singing:
Chorus

"Next comes the running rigging which you're all supposed to know,
'Tis lay aloft, you son-of-a-gun, or overboard you'll go."

HAUL AWAY, JOE

Ukulele tuning: gCEA

Traditional

2. Louie was the King of France afore the revolution,
    Way, haul away, we'll haul away, Joe.
  But then he got his head cut off which spoiled his constitution,
    Way, haul away, we'll haul away, Joe.

3. Once I had a German girl and she was fat and lazy, etc.
  Now I've got a yeller girl, she darn near drives me crazy, etc.

4. St. Patrick was a gentleman, he come from decent people, etc.
  He built a church in Dublin town, and on it put a steeple, etc.

5. Once I was in Ireland a-diggin' turf and praties, etc.
  Now I'm on a lime-juice ship hauling on the braces, etc.

"Haul Away, Joe" is one of a class of sea songs known as Slow-Drag chanteys. These songs typically are short, simple, and were applied to brief tasks of hauling. "Haul On The Bowlin'," which is also included in this collection, provides us with yet another example. The pull on the rope in "Haul Away, Joe" came when the word "Joe" was sung or shouted.

DRUNKEN SAILOR

Ukulele tuning: gCEA

Traditional

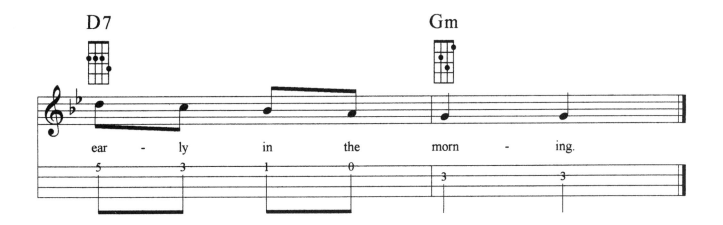

2. Put him in the longboat till he's sober,
   Put him in the longboat till he's sober,
   Put him in the longboat till he's sober,
   Early in the morning.
   Chorus

3. Pull out the plug and wet him all over, (3X)
   Early in the morning.
   Chorus

4. Shave off his belly with a rusty razor, (3X)
   Early in the morning.
   Chorus

5. Put him in the scuppers with a hose pipe on him, (3X)
   Early in the morning.
   Chorus

6. Hoist him up to the topsail yardarm, (3X)
   Early in the morning.
   Chorus

7. Heave him by the leg in a running bowline, (3X)
   Early in the morning.
   Chorus

Three sheets to the wind. *Very drunk. A seafaring expression. Sheets aren't sails, but ropes. These are fixed to the lower corners of sails, to hold them in place. If three sheets are loose and blowing about in the wind then the sails will flap and the boat will lurch about like a drunken sailor. "Maybe you think we were all a sheet in the wind's eye. But I'll tell you I was sober," Long John Silver, Treasure Island 1883*

GOODBYE, MY LOVER, GOODBYE

Ukulele tuning: gCEA

Traditional

The ship is sail - ing down the bay, good - bye, my lov - er, good - bye,____ we

may not meet for man - y a day, good - bye, my lov - er, good - bye.____ My

heart will ev - er more be true, good - bye, my lov - er, good - bye,____ though

now I sad - ly bid you a - dieu, good - bye, my love - er, good - bye. Sing - ing

GOODBYE, MY LOVER, GOODBYE

by - low, my ba - by, by - low, my bounc-ing ba - by boy, sing-ing

by - low, my ba - by, _____ good - bye, my lov - er, good -

bye, good - bye, good - bye, my lov - er, good - bye.

HENRY MARTIN

Ukulele tuning: gCEA

Traditional

2. The lot it fell on Henry Martin,
   The youngest of all of the three,
   That he should turn robber all on the salt sea,
   The salt sea, the salt sea,
   For to maintain his two brothers and he.

3. He had not been sailing but a long winter's night,
   Part of a short winter's day,
   When he espied a stout lofty ship,
   Lofty ship, lofty ship,
   Coming and bearing on down him straight way.

4. "Hello, hello," cried Henry Martin,
   "What makes you sail so nigh?"
   "I'm a rich merchant ship bound for fair London Town,
   London Town, London Town,
   Will you please for to let me pass by?"

5. "Oh no, oh no," cried Henry Martin,
   "That thing it never can be,
   For I have turned robber all on the salt sea,
   The salt sea, the salt, sea,
   For to maintain my two brothers and me."

6. "Then lower your topsail and brail down your mizzen,
   Bow youselves under my lee,
   Or I shall give you a fast-flowing ball,
   Flowing ball, flowing ball,
   And send your dear bodies down in the salt sea."

7. Then broadside to broadside and at it they went,
   For fully two hours or three,
   Till Henry Martin gave to her the death shot,
   The death shot, the death shot,
   Heavily listing to starboard went she.

8. Bad news, bad news, to old England came,
   Bad news to old London Town,
   There's been a rich vessel, and she's cast away,
   Cast away, cast away,
   And all of her merry men drowned.

I NEVER WILL MARRY

Ukulele tuning: gCEA

Traditional

1.One morn-ing I ram-bled____ down by the sea-shore,____ the wind it did whis-tle,____ and the wa-ters did roar.____ I heard a fair maid-en____ give a pit-ti-ful cry,____ it sound-ed so lone-some____ as it swept off on high.____ "I

Chorus:

nev - er will mar - ry,_____ I'll __ be no man's wife,_____ I in-

tend to live sing - le_____ all the days of my life."_____

2. "The shells in the ocean
   Shall be my death bed,
   While the fish in deep water
   Swim over my head."
   Chorus

3. She cast her fair body
   In the water so deep,
   She closed her pretty blue eyes
   Forever to sleep.
   Chorus

NOTE: This sad ballad commemorates a young woman's resolve not to marry
a man she does not love despite the pressure of her parents to do so.

THE ERIE CANAL

Ukulele tuning: gCEA

Traditional

THE ERIE CANAL

2. Gid-dap there, Sal, we passed a lock,
Fifteen miles on the Erie Canal.
We'll make Rome 'bout six o'clock,
Fifteen miles on the Erie Canal.
Just one more trip and back we'll go
Through the rain and sleet and snow,
'Cause every inch of the way we know
From Albany to Buffalo

Constructed between 1817 and 1825, the Erie Canal ran across upstate New York from the Hudson River in Albany to Buffalo, Lake Erie, and the Great Lakes, a distance of about 363 miles. It was a principle route of migration for immigrant settlers and was often referred to as the "Gateway To The West."

THE MARINE'S HYMN

Ukulele tuning: gCEA

Traditional

OVER THE WAVES

(Sobre Las Olas)

Ukulele tuning: gCEA

JUVENTINO ROSAS

No circus would be complete without trapeze acrobats sailing through the air to the accompaniment of this tune.

ON THE BANKS OF THE WABASH

Ukulele tuning: gCEA

PAUL DRESSER